WAR MACHINES

ROCKETS &
MISSILES

by
David West

CRABTREE
PUBLISHING COMPANY
WWW.CRABTREEBOOKS.COM

CRABTREE
PUBLISHING COMPANY
WWW.CRABTREEBOOKS.COM

Author and designer: David West

Illustrator: David West

Editorial director: Kathy Middleton

Editor: Ellen Rodger

Proofreader: Melissa Boyce

**Production coordinator
and Prepress technician**: Ken Wright

Print coordinator: Katherine Berti

Library and Archives Canada Cataloguing in Publication

Title: Rockets and missiles / David West.
Names: West, David, 1956- author.
Description: Series statement: War machines | Includes index.
Identifiers: Canadiana (print) 20190106786 |
    Canadiana (print) 20190106794 |
    Canadiana (ebook) 20190106794 |
    ISBN 9780778766674 (hardcover) |
    ISBN 9780778766827 (softcover) |
    ISBN 9781427124098 (HTML)
Subjects: LCSH: Guided missiles—Juvenile literature. |
    LCSH: Rockets (Ordnance)—Juvenile literature.
Classification: LCC UG1310 .W47 2019 | j623.4/519—dc23

Library of Congress Cataloging-in-Publication Data

Names: West, David, 1956- author.
Title: Rockets and missiles / David West.
Description: New York : Crabtree Publishing Company, [2019]
    Series: War machines | Includes index. |
    Audience: Grades 7-8. | Audience: Ages 10-14 and up. |
Identifiers: LCCN 2019014229 (print) |
    LCCN 2019015895 (ebook) |
    ISBN 9781427124098 (Electronic) |
    ISBN 9780778766674 (hardcover) |
    ISBN 9780778766827 (pbk.)
Subjects: LCSH: Guided missiles--Juvenile literature. |
    Rockets (Ordnance)--Juvenile literature.
Classification: LCC UG1310 (ebook) |
    LCC UG1310 .W47 2019 (print) | DDC 623.4/519--dc23
LC record available at https://lccn.loc.gov/2019014229

Crabtree Publishing Company

www.crabtreebooks.com   1-800-387-7650

Published by Crabtree Publishing Company in 2020

Printed in the U.S.A./072019/CG20190501

**Published in Canada
Crabtree Publishing**
616 Welland Ave.
St. Catharines, ON
L2M 5V6

**Published in the United States
Crabtree Publishing**
PMB 59051, 350 Fifth Ave.
59th Floor,
New York, NY

Contents

Rockets & Missiles

Rockets have been used in warfare since ancient times, when Chinese warriors shot small arrow rockets. By the beginning of the 1800s, modern armies were using iron-cased rockets. The first ones were not very accurate and few hit their targets. Some even looped back on their launchers. However, they did succeed in creating panic among the enemy. By **World War II** (WWII), rockets had become more complex and were being fired from multiple launchers, ships, and aircraft. They were also more stable in flight, but they did not have any form of **homing device** to guide them accurately to their target.

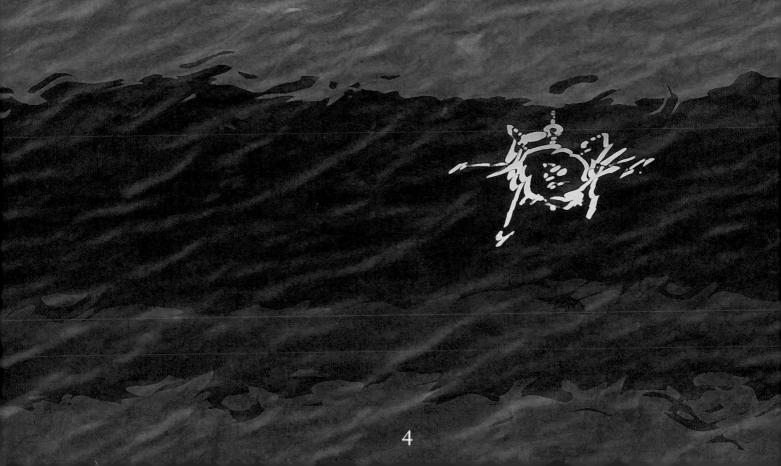

The first guided missiles to follow a curved path were also used during WWII. These missiles had simple **navigation** and targeting devices. Since the end of WWII, missiles have become much more high tech. They now have accurate targeting devices that allow them to hit their marks from a continent away. They can be launched from pads or even submarines hidden under the sea.

A Virginia-class submarine test launches a cruise missile from beneath the waves. Cruise missiles are guided missiles that can be launched from long distances.

The First Rockets

During the 1780s and 1790s, the first iron-cased rockets were used during the **Anglo-Mysore Wars** in southern India. These rockets were used by the **Kingdom of Mysore** to help defeat the army of the **British East India Company** at a battle in 1780.

Mysorean rockets had a range of up to 1.2 miles (1.9 km). Some would burst in the air and others would bounce along the ground. Some had swords attached to **skewer** the enemy. In later battles, the British captured some of these rockets and copied them. British inventor

6

The Second Rocket Troop of the Royal Horse Artillery is shown firing Congreve rockets during the Battle of Waterloo on June 18, 1815. The rockets used sticks to guide them. The rockets helped defeat the French and end the Napoleonic Wars.

William Congreve modeled the rocket named after him on captured Mysorean rockets. Congreve rockets were used by the British to burn the White House during the **War of 1812**. They were also used against the French during the **Napoleonic Wars**. Congreve rockets were used until 1867, when they were replaced by Hale rockets, which did not need wooden guidesticks.

The first rockets used in war were attached to arrows. They may have appeared as early as the 900s C.E. in China. The Munjong Hwacha (right) was used in Korea in 1451. It was one of the first mobile rocket launchers.

WWII Rocket Launchers

Modern rockets were first used during WWII, mainly by the German Army and the **Soviet** Army. The **Allies** used a small number of rocket artillery tanks. Artillery is a type of heavy weapon used to fire at far range. Rockets were used by both sides on ground attack aircraft.

Although not as accurate as traditional artillery, rockets had a number of advantages. They did not need heavy guns to fire them. This meant that their launchers were small enough to mount on trucks. They could fire a

Panzerwerfers were multiple rocket launchers used by the Germans (1). They were transported in a convoy, or group, behind units of Nebelwerfer multiple rocket launchers (2). Here, German soldiers are shown loading them with **high-explosive warheads**.

number of explosives at the same time, which increased the enemy's sense of shock and fear. The sound they made as they neared their target resulted in the nickname "moaning minnies." Since the rocket launchers were mobile, they could quickly change position using a **tactic** known as "shoot and scoot." This allowed them to escape detection by the enemy.

Soviet Katyusha rockets were launched from trucks. The rockets made a howling sound that terrified enemy soldiers.

1

WWII Shoulder Launchers

Antitank rocket launchers were first used during WWII. They were carried by infantry, the part of the army that goes into combat on foot. The United States Army used the "bazooka," also called a "stovepipe," as an antitank weapon. It was named after a musical instrument.

Fired from the shoulder, bazookas used a high-explosive antitank (HEAT) warhead. It was **propelled** by a rocket. Bazookas were operated by a two-person team. A loader inserted the rocket and an operator fired the

U.S. troops fire an antitank missile from a bazooka (1) at a Tiger tank during the Battle of the Bulge (December 16, 1944–January 25, 1945). The battle was a German attempt to defeat the Allies in Belgium. It was the bloodiest battle of the war for U.S. troops.

weapon. The loader had to be sure not to position himself directly behind the bazooka. The warhead was capable of piercing **armor plate**. The bazooka was also used against other armored vehicles, machine gun nests, and **bunkers**. The chemical white phosphorus (WP) was used to create smoke screens and drive enemies out of bunkers and dugouts.

During WWII, German forces captured several bazookas in North Africa and **Eastern Front** battles. They copied the design for their own weapon, called the Panzerschreck ("tank terror").

Air-to-Surface

The earliest air-to-surface missiles (ASMs) appeared during WWII. The British RP-3s and the U.S. High Velocity Aircraft Rockets (HVARs) were attached to various aircraft. Their high-explosive warheads could knock the turret off a Tiger tank.

These early missiles were launched from aircraft at targets on land or sea. They were propelled, or fired, by rockets and were not guided. Four tail fins spun the rocket, making it stable in flight. It was difficult

A pair of British Royal Air Force (RAF) Hawker Typhoon aircraft attack a column of German tanks. The tanks are retreating from France in mid-August 1944, during WWII. The Typhoons are using RP-3 rockets.

to be accurate, as the angle of attack and the air speed had to be precise. ASMs were only effective in the hands of skilled, experienced pilots. HVARs were widely used in the **Korean War** (1950–1953). Today, ASMs are guided by sophisticated technology. They are highly accurate.

The AGM-65 Maverick, shown here being fired from an F-16, has a range of over 13.7 miles (22 km). It has a solid-fuel rocket engine and is locked onto its target by the pilot. It is used against tanks, ships, and air defenses.

3

Early Guided Missiles

The first guided missiles were developed by Germany during WWII. The V-1 flying bomb was an early cruise missile that used a pulse-jet engine. The V-2, launched in 1944, was the world's first long-range guided **ballistic missile**. It was powered by a **liquid-propellant engine**.

When launched, the V-2 rocket propelled itself for 65 seconds, reaching a height of 50 miles (80 km). After the engine shut down, it continued its path to its target. It was guided by four rudders on the tail fins, and

14

A V-2 rocket on a trailer called a Meillerwagen (1) has arrived at its launch site in a forest in Germany. Military personnel run to raise it to a vertical position on a firing stand called a Brennstand (2). A Hanomag SS-100 (3) was often used to tow the missile to the launch site.

four internal rudders at the exit of the motor. Early models used a simple computer to keep it on course. The missile could be launched anywhere, such as from roads running through forests. Special trailers and mobile launch wagons, along with fuel tanks, were required for each launch.

The V-1 used an autopilot and a gyrocompass to control its flight. It could be launched from a ramp pointing in the right direction. A counter measured the distance the weapon flew.

3

2

Air-to-Air

Air-to-air missiles (AAMs) are fired from one aircraft to destroy another. Some are short range, meaning they are effective at less than 18.6 miles (30 km). These are usually heat-seeking missiles. Others are medium- to long-range missiles that are guided by **radar**.

Modern fighter aircraft use air-to-air missiles. The AIM-9 Sidewinder was first used by the U.S. Navy. It is a short-range air-to-air missile that was first used in 1956. Most modern air forces still use a form of these today.

16

The first-ever combat use of the American-made Sidewinder air-to-air missiles was in 1958. Here, two Republic of China Air Force F-86 Sabres (1) fire the missiles (2) at People's Republic of China MiG-17s (3). Today, the Sidewinder is still a widely used missile.

The most high-tech ones are contrast and infrared homing devices, or seekers. The weapons guidance systems on these use electromagnetic radiation from a target to track and follow it. This radiation is heat or light that is beyond visual range, meaning it cannot be seen with the human eye. Many things, such as vehicles or people, emit heat—making them easy targets.

Air-to-air unguided rockets were first carried in **World War I** (WWI) on biplanes like this Nieuport.

Antitank

Antitank guided missile (ATGM) launchers range in size. Some are shoulder-launch weapons, which can be transported by a single soldier. Others are vehicle- and aircraft-mounted missile systems. Some tanks can also fire ATGMs from their guns.

ATGMs were developed during the 1950s. An operator uses a joystick to steer the missile to its target. With second-generation ATGMs, the operator uses a sighting device to eye the target. Electronics in the

This antitank guided missile is Tube-launched, Optically tracked, and Wire-guided (TOW). It was fired from a Wiesel Armored Weapons Carrier (AWC) during Exercise Reforger, a military operation during the **Cold War** in 1982.

missile guide it to the target. Modern guidance systems use a laser infrared camera or radar in the nose of the missile. These systems are called "fire-and-forget" since they make their own way to the target. Most ATGMs have high-explosive antitank (HEAT) warheads. They are designed specifically for penetrating armor.

This portable missile launcher is firing a Javelin fire-and-forget ATGM. The missile flies above its target and then shoots down on the thinner armor of the upper surfaces of a tank.

1

Surface-to-Air

Surface-to-air missile (SAM) or ground-to-air missile (GTAM) launchers are used by armies to protect ground forces from attack by aircraft. Developed during the 1950s, guided antiaircraft missiles became a serious threat to **supersonic** jet aircraft during the **Vietnam War** (1955–1975).

By the early 1960s, SAMs had shown that in combat, high-speed, high-altitude flight was deadly. SAMs adapted to the the tactics pilots

20

A Pantsir-S1 unit (1) of the Syrian Armed Forces uses an F7E6 surface-to-air missile to down a Turkish Air Force F-4 Phantom II (2) over the Syrian coast on June 22, 2012.

used, including flying below the line-of-sight of missiles' radar systems. Over time, the missiles became smaller, and were mounted on light armored vehicles, making them mobile. Some, like the U.S. Blowpipe, can even be fired from portable launch tubes called MANPADS (Man-Portable Air-Defense System).

The S-75 Dvina was the first surface-to-air missile to down a plane. It shot down a Taiwanese Martin RB-57D Canberra over China in 1959.

2-A-202   ARMADA

1

2

Antiship

Antiship missiles (ASMs) are guided missiles used against ships and small boats. They use various navigation aids, such as radar or infrared technology, to zero in on their target. They can be launched from land, or from warships, submarines, bombers, fighter planes, and helicopters.

Most antiship missiles fly close to the surface of the ocean so that they can avoid detection by enemy radar. The Exocet missile can be launched 43.5

22

One of a pair of Argentinian air force Super Etendards (1) fires an Exocet antiship missile (2), sinking the Royal Navy destroyer HMS *Sheffield* on May 4, 1982, during the **Falklands War**.

miles (70 km) from its target. It flies 3.3–6.6 feet (1–2 m) above the ocean's surface. Ships are armed with SAM missiles, such as the Sea Dart, to shoot down antiship missiles. Modern warship designs use stealth technology to hide from enemy missile attacks.

Radio-controlled antiship missiles were first used during WWII. The German Luftwaffe (air force) used the Henschel Hs 293 against Allied warships in the Mediterranean Sea.

3

Mobile Ballistic Missiles

Mobile ballistic missiles are usually ballistic missiles designed for short-range battlefield use. They often have a range of less than 186 miles (300 km). They are called tactical ballistic missiles (TBMs) or battlefield range ballistic missiles (BRBMs).

The quick deployment of a mobile TBM allows the launcher to fire its missile and then return to a hidden location. During the Gulf War, Iraqi Scud launch missiles were timed in 30-minute sequences.

Iraqi forces fire a Scud missile (1) during the Gulf War as a second launcher prepares its missile (2). A third Scud launcher (3) continues along a desert road to its launch location.

This allowed the Iraqis to avoid enemy air strikes. The missiles can carry a variety of warheads, from conventional high-explosive to nuclear.

Mobile launchers are sometimes used to launch intercontinental ballistic missiles (ICBMs). These are missiles with a minimum range of 3,418 miles (5,500 km) that are designed to deliver nuclear warheads. The Topol-M, shown here, is a Russian three-stage ICBM. It can carry four to six warheads. The mobile launcher can travel through rough terrain and launch its missile from anywhere.

1

2

STORMSHADOW
SERIAL NO 004
DE TON TRITON V
INTEG D CHASSIS
LOT NO DDF 104-0

Cruise Missiles

Cruise missiles are designed to strike a target over long distances with great precision. They are self-navigating and use a number of different guidance systems. Cruise missiles can travel lightning fast at low altitudes to avoid radar detection.

Cruise missiles can be launched from ground launchers, aircraft, surface ships, or submarines. They can carry either a conventional or nuclear warhead. Supersonic cruise missiles are powered by a ramjet engine.

An RAF Tornado (1) releases a pair of Storm Shadow cruise missiles (2) during the 2003 **invasion of Iraq**. A second Tornado (3) is still carrying its Storm Shadows under its fuselage.

Subsonic cruise missiles, such as the Storm Shadow, are powered by a turbojet and can travel 348 miles (560 km). Storm Shadow is a fire-and-forget missile, programmed before launch. It is guided by GPS and terrain mapping. Near its target, it releases its nose cone to reveal a high-resolution camera. If it cannot locate its target, it will crash in a safe place to avoid unintended casualties.

The Tomahawk cruise missile can be launched from ships or submarines. It can travel 1,553 miles (2,500 km).

1

Antiballistic Missiles

Antiballistic missiles (ABMs) are surface-to-air missiles designed to knock out ballistic missiles. Ballistic missiles are used to deliver many kinds of warheads, including nuclear and chemical warheads.

The Arrow 3 is one of only three systems that can intercept ICBMs. It is designed to intercept the enemy's ICBM in space. The Arrow 3 can switch directions and even destroy satellites. The missile has a range of up to 1,491 miles (2,400 km). Smaller missiles, such as the

28

A U.S. Army Patriot system fires a missile during the 2003 invasion of Iraq. The system consists of the fire control section, radar set, and engagement control station (1), antenna mast group (2) and launchers (3). All are trailer mounted.

U.S. Army's Patriot missile long-range air defense system, are used against tactical ballistic missiles. The radar set and launchers are mounted on trailers which are towed by powerful M983 trucks. The system was used against Iraqi Scud missiles during the Iraq War.

Long-range surface-to-air missile systems like this Russian SA-10 Grumble can shoot down fast-flying drones and cruise missiles. Later models were developed to intercept ballistic missiles.

Missile Specs

More information on the rockets and missiles in this book

Nebelwerfer rocket
Type: SSM, high-explosive warhead
Length: 11.8 feet (3.6 m)
Range: 4.9 miles (7.85 km)

Congreve rocket
Type: SSM, high-explosive warhead
Length: 16.2 feet (5 m) with stick
Range: 900 feet (274.3 m)

M6A1 bazooka-fired rocket
Type: HEAT warhead
Length: 2 feet (0.6 m)
Range: 1,214 feet (370 m)

RP-3
Type: ASM, high-explosive warhead
Length: 4.6 feet (1.4 m)
Range: 1 mile (1.6 km)

AIM-9 Sidewinder
Type: AAM, high-explosive fragmentation warhead
Length: 9.8 feet (3 m)
Range: 22 miles (35.4 km)

MIM-104 Patriot
Type: ABM, high-explosive fragmentation warhead
Length: 19 feet (5.8 m)
Range: 21.7 miles (35 km)

TOW missile
Type: ATGM, HEAT warhead
Length: 3.9 feet (1.2 m)
Range: 2.3 miles (3.7 km)

57E6 missile
Type: SAM, high-explosive fragmentation warhead
Length: 10.5 feet (3.2 m)
Range: 12.4 miles (20 km)

Exocet
Type: ASM, high-explosive fragmentation warhead or semi-armor piercing
Length: 15.4 feet (4.7 m)
Range: 43.5 miles (70 km)

Scud
Type: TBM, high-explosive, nuclear, or chemical warhead
Length: 37 feet (11.3 m)
Range: 435 miles (700 km)

Storm Shadow
Type: Air-launched cruise missile, multistage warhead
Length: 16.7 feet (5.1 m)
Range: 344.8 miles (555 km)

V-2
Type: Long-range guided ballistic missile, high-explosive warhead
Length: 45.9 feet (14 m)
Range: 198.8 miles (320 km)

Glossary

Allies The nations that fought against Nazi Germany and the Axis powers during World War II

Anglo-Mysore Wars A series of wars fought in the late 1700s between the Kingdom of Mysore in India and the British East India Company

armor plate A piece of hardened steel used to cover tanks, aircraft, or ships

ballistic missile A missile with a high, arcing path

British East India Company A British trading company that seized control over large parts of India and Southeast Asia

bunkers Fortified underground protection

Cold War (1947–1991) The name of the politically hostile relationship between the United States and the Soviet Union after World War II

Eastern Front A front line of conflict during World War II (1939–1945), between the Allies and Nazi Germany in eastern Europe

Falklands War (1982) A war between Argentina and the United Kingdom over island territory off the coast of Argentina

high-explosive warheads A type of explosive delivered in a rocket that can penetrate thick armor

homing device Machinery used to guide to a destination

invasion of Iraq The first stage of the Iraq War in 2003 in which forces from the United States, the United Kingdom, Australia, and Poland invaded Iraq

Kingdom of Mysore A former kingdom in southern India, founded in 1399

Korean War (1950–1953) A war between North Korea, supported by China and the Soviet Union, and South Korea, supported by the United States and the United Nations

liquid-propellant engine A rocket engine that uses liquid fuel

Napoleonic Wars (1803–1815) A series of conflicts between France, led by Napoleon Bonaparte, and various European powers

navigation Plotting and determining the course of ships, aircraft, or missiles

propelled Driven forward

radar A detection system that uses radio waves to calculate the range of objects

Second Taiwan Strait Crisis (1958) A conflict between the People's Republic of China and the Republic of China (Taiwan) over territory

skewer To pierce with a sharp object

Soviet Referring to the Soviet Union (1922–1991), a union of states in Eastern Europe and Asia

subsonic Less than the speed of sound

supersonic Greater than the speed of sound

Syrian Civil War (2011–present) A war between the government of Syria and a number of opposing groups within the same country

tactic A plan or method used to accomplish a goal

Vietnam War (1955–1975) A conflict between North Vietnam and its allies, China and the Soviet Union, and South Vietnam and its allies, the United States, South Korea, Australia, and the Philippines

War of 1812 (1812–1815) A war between the United States and Great Britain in its colonies in North America

World War I (1914–1918) An international conflict fought mainly in Europe and the Middle East, between the Central powers, including Austria-Hungary, Germany, and the Ottoman Empire, and the Allies, including the United Kingdom, Canada, Australia, and later, the United States

World War II (1939–1945) An international conflict fought in Europe, Asia, and Africa, between the Axis powers, including Germany, Italy, and Japan, and the Allies, including the United Kingdom, France, Canada, Australia, and in 1941, the United States

Index